French-Canadian Roots

Researching Your French Canadian Family Tree and Genealogy

By Lawrence Compagna

Expanded Third Edition (paperback, in full color)

Copyright 2017

ISBN: 978-1-387-37075-7

Published by the Candco Corporation

French-Canadian Roots

The author has traced thousands of his direct ancestors, all the way into the middle ages, and arguably right back into antiquity. Using methods described in this book you can do the same, through your French Canadian ancestors, whose pedigrees are some of the best documented on the planet. The instructions are step-by-step, with tips on what to look for and how to progress rapidly. Your kin are waiting to be discovered and this book will help you find them.

French-Canadian Roots

Dedicated to my mother for encouraging me, Roseanne for opening the door, Madison for showing me how to be creative, Conrad for the intellectual stimulation, and finally to Wyatt ... who forever inspires me

French-Canadian Roots

Table of Contents

Preface

I have a confession to make: I'm 100% French, but I don't speak the language.

To be more accurate: All of my ancestors were French, or French Canadian, but I'm a Canadian / American. Also, for the sake of honesty, I did take French up to high school but I learned very little from it. It wasn't a reflection of my teachers; I just don't have a knack for languages.

Up until about ten years ago my lack of French fluency didn't bother me at all. I was able to get a college degree and my career was solid. But all that changed when my passion for genealogy was born.

Introduction

My name is Lawrence. I'm an average guy, at least I think I'm average; I'm a white collar professional by day, three children, and my home is unspectacular. Even my passion for genealogy is kind of average; I read somewhere that researching one's ancestors is one of the most popular pursuits on the internet.

What isn't average is what I've done with my passion for genealogy: I traced thousands of direct ancestors and pushed my line back beyond the middle ages, arguably right back into antiquity.

Before I tell you about that, and provide some advice so that you can do the same, let me tell you about how I got started.

One day my cousin Roseanne was visiting my house. After describing her recent trip to Quebec, she unfolded a piece of paper and laid it down on the coffee table in front of me. I picked it up and perused it. What I was looking at was a chart showing my namesake ancestors and their wives going back to the early 17th Century. Each generation was listed, I think there were ten. At the top of the chart was my great, great …. Keep going for eight times or so, grandfather Mathias.

I was astounded. We knew our ancestors going back into the 1600's? I didn't know this was possible. This was at a time when the internet was still relatively young having been born a decade or so earlier. Its use in genealogy was still in its infancy as well, and most genealogical research was still done the old and hard way: in person at archives. This is what my cousin had done. She had a few photocopies to go along with the hand drawn chart I was looking at now. One was particularly interesting. It was a ship's manifest from the year 1664. In that year Mathias came to the new world aboard the Black Holland.

Mathias was among the first Europeans in the America's and as I would realize later it was for this reason that our descent from him was remembered … because he did something spectacular. He came to an alien world called America where life was harsh and often ended up with a cruel ending at the hands of the natives who were desperately trying to stem the flow of white people invading their lands.

After Roseanne left I became fascinated with the chart. It only listed my namesake line, was it possible to flesh out my entire family tree? Even more intriguing: was it

French-Canadian Roots

possible to push my ancestry beyond Mathias into the 16th century or even beyond?

My obsession was born.

You

If you're reading this I assume a few things about you: One, you have French Canadian ancestors. Two: You may or may not speak French. Thirdly, you have a passion for genealogy.

If this describes you then you're in luck. It's quite likely that I'll succeed in helping you uncover your royal ancestors. Your ancestry will be pushed back to the Holy Roman Emperor Charlemagne and you'll uncover all sorts of interesting characters along the way.

You'll discover that you have ancestors who were murdered, some by the Iroquois (the arch enemy of the early French Canadian settlers). Others were hung, committed terrible crimes, and many had land disputes that went before the courts. For most of our ancestors it is only by their infamy that we have any information on them as court records survive from that time, whereas the deeds of your good ancestors went unrecorded and thus we know little about them.

You'll soon realize that you're fortunate to have French Canadian ancestors; as one astute volunteer from the gargantuan Family History Library in Salt Lake City told me: "You're lucky to have ancestors from Quebec because they have among the best records in the world." I also read somewhere that the records of French Canadians are second in the world only to those of Iceland. For Europeans descendants at least, I believe this to be true.

Three quarters of my ancestry is French Canadian, the other quarter emigrated from France to Canada via Ellis Island in 1905. After great success with my Canadian ancestors I thought that the French side would be a treasure trove. I was wrong. As mentioned earlier, our descent from people who have done great things is remembered. The Canadians descended from people like Mathias who were colonizing an alien world. My French ancestors were grape farmers who had no such notable people in their family tree. Furthermore Europe was repeatedly decimated by war, whereas Canada never suffered this fate. For example, before retreating from the French city of Caen, the Nazis burnt the archives to the ground. It contained 14,000 books relating to the ancestry of Caen's inhabitants.

French-Canadian Roots

What I discovered (the hard way) is that it is often impossible to trace the lineage of commoners in France more than a few hundred years. At the very least, it is difficult.

You're lucky if you have French Canadian ancestors.

The New World

It was like going to Mars.

Except it wasn't Mars your ancestor was going to, it was the new world. And they weren't just visiting there; they were going to colonize this alien place. But this other world was already inhabited; by people whom they mistakenly called "Indians", and some of them did not like seeing the pasty white faces of your ancestors. Some, like the Iroquois, were in league with the other European superpower trying to control this world. They were allied with the English who had deemed their part of the new world "New England" just as your ancestors called yours "New France".

Though the number of colonists of English origin far outnumbered those of French, the land called New France encompassed not only Canada, but the middle of the United States as well. There were three major parts to France's

13

dominion: Acadia, New France proper, and Louisiana. The latter was the biggest area by size, whereas New France was the biggest by population. Populations were small though. During the first census in 1666 the population of Quebec, the largest city in the dominion, was just 6,000 people. Most of the people were men, though the proportion of women was increasing through a program called "the King's Daughters." These were young women of good character who had fallen on hard times, usually due to the death of their father. Sometimes they were orphans. They came to the new world with a dowry provided by the king himself. Marriages took place soon after their arrival, though they had a brief period where they could annul the arrangement and seek a new husband.

There was a lot to survive in the new world if you made it there at all. A significant portion of the colonists died on the long voyage due to storms and disease. If you made it through that, there was a good chance that you would die from scurvy, from an assault by the Iroquois, or at the hands of the English.

What motivated our ancestors to colonize this hostile world? Unlike the English colony religious freedom was not part of the deal: you had to be Roman Catholic. After a hundred years of fighting between the Protestants and Catholics in France, the former had been crushed. It's quite likely that most of your ancestors had at one time been members of a Protestant group called "Huguenots". But after the Siege of La Rochelle in 1628 the Huguenots were all but destroyed and those that remained were eventually compelled to become Catholic or die. Since you're here, you are most likely descended from those who chose to live as Catholics.

The French port city of La Rochelle itself, and the outlying province of Aunis, was the source of most of your ancestors. Aunis is in the ancient region known as Aquitaine which alternated between French and English ownership. If you visit La Rochelle you'll probably be surprised by how beautiful it and the countryside are. Aside from the constant warring and religious intolerance why would your ancestor leave this gorgeous place?

French-Canadian Roots

Some of your ancestors were most likely thrill seekers, but we have no direct evidence of this compelling people to leave for the new world. The right answer is land.

Historically land in Western Europe could only be owned by members of the noble class. Though some of your ancestors most likely belonged to that class of people, it is more likely that they were commoners. They were peasants devoid of the right to own land. Furthermore, they couldn't carry a sword as this too was the right of a nobleman. But in the new world both were possible.

So your ancestor jumped on a boat, sailed for six weeks, and arrived in a place like Quebec City. If he was too poor to finance his own journey he was indentured. An indentured servant is one step above being a slave. They had rights, but for a period of time they had to serve their master, the person who financed their journey. After a number of years they were free to establish a homestead, land of their own where they could build a house, keep livestock and farm. Being armed was crucial, because they also had to defend themselves from the ever present risk of an Iroquois raid.

Kidnapping was also a risk of life in the new world, with all of the parties involved (French, English, natives) carrying each other's citizens off and ransoming. Some of those kidnapped chose to stay with the kidnappers. A small number of your French Canadian ancestors have English last names. They were most likely taken from New England as children, eventually freed, but chose to remain in New France where they ended up marrying French women and men and raising families.

The families were huge in New France. Not just because they were Catholic, but because the state had decreed it. As a father and mother you were fined if your daughter was 16, living with you, and … (gasp) unmarried. A similar fine was levied if you had a son in a similar circumstance. Consequently people married young back then. It was not uncommon for a girl to be married at 13 or 14. Men would marry young too, but for them there was an expectation that they could support a family. Young couples in their early twenties had a large brood of kids already.

Disease was a constant companion. Small pox killed huge numbers of people. Sometimes it would claim multiple family members in a single season. Infant mortality kept parents in perpetual grief.

French-Canadian Roots

By 1759 France's time in the new world was all but over. On the Plains of Abraham the principle city of Quebec was lost to the English and never retaken. The consequence of this loss was that it stemmed the tide of French colonists coming to the new world. The indirect consequence, and why it is relevant in the context of this book, is that any French Canadian ancestors that you have invariably had to have been in Canada by 1700, or in other words you are assuredly descended from the first white settlers of North America.

They did something special these ancestors of yours. They traveled to a "Mars like" world, survived it, and eventually thrived. They were the pioneers, and the fathers and mothers of the country. It is for this reason that they are remembered, and it is for this reason that we - their descendants - can trace our family trees so well.

If you were here with me right now, I'd raise my wine glass in the air and propose a toast: "To our ancestors!"

Your Tool Kit

Your computer will be your best friend in this quest. You'll not only use the internet, but you'll soon need a database program to manage the vast numbers of ancestors that you're going to uncover. Your tool kit will consist of the following:

- One computer with decent processing speed and RAM.
- Access to the internet.
- One software genealogy software program. I recommend Legacy.
- Proficiency in Gedcom downloads (I'll get to this later.)
- An online translation tool. (like Google Translate)
- One first class plane ticket to France.
- Another first class plane ticket to Quebec.

Note: if your partner wants to join you, make it two plane tickets, though they are going to have to sit quietly while you analyze records in the archives for hours at a time (and may have to fly economy because you only have enough money for one first class ticket). Also note that the plane tickets are optional. The truth is that most of what is in the archives of France and Quebec is available on the internet, largely thanks to the efforts of the Church of Latter Day Saints who have gone to great lengths to copy and safeguard genelogical records.

French-Canadian Roots

You may also find it easier to work with records on the internet than in an archive, simply because you can often copy and paste what you find into a translation program such as Google Translate and get a quick French to English version of what you're reading. You can't do this with the actual document in an archive.

Resources

Now that you know what to put in your toolkit let's examine the resources available to you. To do so, we will divide them between those that are online, and those that are not.

Offline

Before you can use online research tools to push your pedigree back into the 17th Century and beyond you need to establish your more recent family tree without the use of a computer. It's unlikely that you'll find your ancient ancestors without knowing the specifics about the ones who weren't so ancient.

To do this talk to the elder members of your clan and find out what they know and what they have. Do they have a family history book? Do they have any birth, death, marriage or baptismal records? What do they remember about their grandparents? When talking to them bear in mind that you're in search of the where, when, and what of your forbearers: you want legal names (including middle), precise birth, death, and marriage dates, and the location of these events as well as that of where they resided. Carefully record this information even if it's only an allegation. Allegations are often true, though you should earmark these as such until they are proven.

Once you have a good idea of whom your great-grand parents were you are ready to push your ancestry back into the 19th Century and beyond using the internet.

Online

Online resources are plentiful. The starting point in your continuing search is the Rootsweb WorldConnect Project due to the availability of GEDCOM files on this site and the ease with which you can download them. GEDCOM files allow you to get a running start by downloading the work of other genealogists. In order to get this running start you must purchase a software package that is capable of loading them. A leader in this area is Legacy Family Tree. You can purchase their product online and download the program. From that point you can trace your French Canadian ancestors on Rootsweb, find pedigrees that have a GEDCOM available, and download a part of your pedigree.

Legacy software can be purchased on the web at:

legacyfamilytree.com/downloadlegacy.asp

You can download a free version to begin with, but you'll soon find that the reasonable cost of the deluxe version makes it a good value proposition.

Once you have that software access Rootsweb on the web at:

http://wc.rootsweb.ancestry.com/cgi-bin/igm.cgi

The combination of Rootsweb, GEDCOMS and Legacy software will quickly yield a large portion of your French Canadian Family tree. You'll need other online resources to fill in gaps in your tree. The two leading resources for this purpose are Ancestry and the University of Montreal. Both sites require a fee, but it is reasonable and once again, a great value. The latter site, known as the PRDH (a French acronym for "The Research Program in Historical Demography" of the University of Montreal) can be accessed at:

genealogie.umontreal.ca/en/home

Thankfully (for us Anglophones), the site has an English portal. Here you'll find seemingly every legal and church document concerning your ancestors prior to the 19th Century. This provides you a snapshot of your ancestor's whereabouts, family, and dealings (including land transactions).

Ancestry.com allows the user to access the extensive records collection maintained by the Church of Latter Day Saints. They've gone to great lengths to scan genealogical records not only in Canada and the USA, but all over the world. If you have a gap in your family tree you're likely to uncover photographs of birth certificates, marriage certificates, and baptismal records in their database. You can then download them, and flesh out your family tree. However, this will only work for ancestors who've been deceased for at least thirty years or so.

Though both sites are in English, most of the records you encounter will be in French only. Use an online translation tool like Google Translate or Babelfish to help you understand what you're looking at.

Lastly you'll need to use the GFNA - Quebec Royal Descends website to help you search for ancestors who were, or may have been, members of the French nobility. French nobility is the key to pushing your genealogy back into the middle ages.

Discover Your Pedigree

Let's play make believe.

You've heard a rumor from a relative that you are a remote cousin of Canadian Prime Minister Justin Trudeau. This stimulates your interest in learning about your family tree. Is it true or not? Aside from Justin, do you have any other notable ancestors? Then you start to think about these mysterious people. Who were they? Where did they come from? Where did they live? What did they do for a living?

Step One – Your Great Grandparents

And now you're looking for advice on how to uncover these mysterious ancestors of yours. The first thing you need to do is determine who your great grand-parents were. So you talk to an Aunt who shares what will soon become

25

your obsession. She has a book that shows that one of your great grand-parents was named Jean Charles Emile Trudeau. He was born way back in 1874. He represents 1/8th of your total pedigree because you have seven other great grand-grandparents. You're going to have to repeat the process that follows for eight of them, but for now (and for the purposes of this book) you will trace the lineage of Jean Charles only.

Step Two – Rootsweb and GEDCOM

As mentioned earlier the second step to perform after you've established your ancestors into the 19th Century is to look for a pedigree on Rootsweb that has a downloadable GEDCOM. You already followed my earlier advice and bought a genealogy database that will serve as your repository for these GEDCOM files as well as your own personal research. On your computer you type in:

wc.rootsweb.ancestry.com/cgi-bin/igm.cgi

RootsWeb's WorldConnect Project
Global Search

Names: 831,433,927 Surnames: 6,431,090 Databases: 446,360

Surname		Exact	Father	
Given Name		omit living	Mother	
Birth Place		omit blanks	Spouse	
Birth Year	Exact		Skip Database	
Death Place		omit blanks	Updated Within	Forever
Death Year	Exact		Has Descendants	
Marriage Place		omit blanks	Has Notes	
Marriage Year	Exact		Has Sources	

Fuzzy Search ☐ (uses soundex)   Search   Reset

In the surname field you enter "Trudeau", and in the Given name simply "Jean". The result of your query is daunting:

over 1,000 records representing an assortment of individuals from four different centuries and several countries. You'll need to be more specific. All you know about Jean's wife, your grandmother, was that her name was Grace. You type that into the Spouse field (see Figure 1). The result is startling. The list of results is reduced from over 1,000 to just two (see Figure 2). Furthermore the birth date for both records says "After 1874", and you happen to know that your great grandfather was born in 1876. Eureka!

Figure 1:

RootsWeb's WorldConnect Project
Global Search

Names: 831,018,000 Surnames: 6,428,151 Databases: 446,309

Surname	trudeau		Exact	Father	
Given Name	Jean		☐ omit living	Mother	
Birth Place			☐ omit blanks	Spouse	grace
Birth Year		Exact		Skip Database	
Death Place			☐ omit blanks	Updated Within	Forever
Death Year		Exact		☐ Has Descendants	
Marriage Place			☐ omit blanks	☐ Has Notes	
Marriage Year		Exact		☐ Has Sources	

Fuzzy Search ☐ (uses soundex)   Search   Reset

Figure 2:

RootsWeb's WorldConnect Project
Global Search

Names: 831,018,000 Surnames: 6,428,151 Databases: 446,309

Results 1-2 of 2

| Name | Birth/Christening | | Death/Burial | | Database | Order record? | Other Matches |
	Date	Place	Date	Place			
Trudeau, Jean Charles Emile	AFT 1874				gs55meandu		Census Newspapers Military Cemetery
Father: Joseph Trudeau Mother: Marie Malvina Cardinal Spouse: Grace Elliott							
Trudeau, Jean Charles Emile	AFT 1874				gta-1		Census Newspapers Military Cemetery
Father: Joseph Trudeau Mother: Marie Malvina Cardinal Spouse: Grace Elliott							

Figure 3:

Index | **Descendancy** | **Register** | **Pedigree** | **Ahnentafel** | **Download GEDCOM** |

- *ID:* I10155
- *Name:* **Jean Charles Emile TRUDEAU**
- *Sex:* M
- *Birth:* AFT 1874

Figure 4:

Download full GEDCOM as a ZIP file

Starting with	I10155
Name	Jean Charles Emile TRUDEAU
Born	AFT 1874 in
Died	in
Produce a GEDCOM file from	Ancestors
Number of Generations	10
End of line character	CRLF

Download

Does either record have a GEDCOM available? You're in
luck. Clicking on each record shows that both do (see
Figure 3). Which one should you choose? You click on the
"Download GEDCOM" on each page. One reveals that the
number of generations available to download is ten (see
Figure 4), while the other is six. You're probably going to
want to download the larger file but before that examine the
quality of the tree by examining a sample of individuals in
each tree. Which has better sourcing? Which has more
extensive information, and which has more ancestors
shown? You pick the second record for a number of
reasons: you can download ten generations, the number of
ancestors shown exceeds that of the first even in the first

six generations shown, and it goes further back (see figure 5).

Figure 5:

```
                                               /Jean VARIN d: 1665
                                         /Catherine VARIN b: ABT 1645 d: 27 JAN 1705
                                         |      \Jeanne BOUCHE
                                 \Anne Marie TESSIER b: 7 MAY 1692 d: 3 JAN 1750
                                               /Philippe AMYOT(AMIOT) b: 1602 d: 26 SEP 1636
                                 /Mathieu Amyot Sieur DE VILLENEUVE b: 23 MAY 1628 d: 19 DEC 1688
                                 |             /Guillaume Couvent\Couvent dit ESTREE b: 1574 d: BEF 1651 =>
                                 |       \Anne COUVENT\COUVENT b: 1601 d: 25 DEC 1675
                                 |                 \Antoinette DE LONGUEVAL\LONGVAL b: 1580 =>
                         \Jeanne Anne Marie Amyot dit VILLENEUVE b: 22 NOV 1670 d: 11 FEB 1748
                                 |             /Issac MIVILLE
                                 /Pierre Miville dit LE SUISSE b: 1602 d: 14 OCT 1669
                                 |       \Salome LOMENIE
                         \Marie Anne MIVILLE b: 13 DEC 1652 d: 5 SEP 1702
                                 |             /Aphonse MAUGIS\MONGIS
                                 \Charlotte MAUGIS\MONGIS\MAUGER b: 1609 d: 10 OCT 1676
                                               \Louise DE MERLE
                 /Amable Rene Gagne dit BELEVANCE b: 27 SEP 1759 d: BEF 14 OCT 1811
                 |       /Marie Catherine LONGTIN b: 2 SEP 1723 d: 12 AUG 1778
                 \Marguerite GAGNE b: 22 MAR 1781
                         \Marie HAMELIN b: 3 JUL 1763 d: BEF 16 JUL 1821
 /Joseph TRUDEAU b: AFT 1838
 |               /Louis DUPUIS
 |       /Michel-Nicolas DUPUIS b: 14 NOV 1788
 |       |       \Marguerite GUICHON
 |       \Marie Louise DUPUIS b: 20 APR 1817 d: BEF 1 OCT 1850
 |               /Henri-Hyacinthe BOIRE
 |       \Josephte BOIRE b: 10 APR 1790
 |               \Marguerite BERTHIAUME
Jean Charles Emile TRUDEAU b: AFT 1974
 |               /Pierre CARDINAL
 |       /Soline CARDINAL b: AFT 1815
 |       |       \Anne Ste. MARIE
 \Marie Malvina CARDINAL b: 1849
         \Marguerite Suprenant ditte LAFONTAINE
```

I'm sitting right next to you and I point out that the decision is not mutually exclusive. You can download both, but you have to be careful because doing so could lead to a large number of duplicate entries requiring a lot of clean up. I suggest that you proceed with the download of the second record after which we'll discuss what we should do with the other record. You're a little nervous, but you click on "Download GEDCOM".

"Don't worry" I tell you. "You can't break anything." *At this point,* I think to myself,

You accept all of the default settings and click "Download." A few seconds later the information now resides on your hard drive.

Next I tell you to open your genealogy database program. For our purposes the one you purchased was Legacy

Family Tree. You've already done the tutorial, but the database itself is empty. You haven't even put yourself, your parents, or your grandparents in it yet. With my guidance you open File<Import<GEDCOM and proceed with the import. A panel opens up stating that 328 individuals from 200 families are included. Accepting all of the defaults you click on "Start the import." A message tells you that you've been successful, and asks if you want to merge duplicates now. The answer is no, but after you import the other GEDCOM you'll click yes and follow the directions.

Congratulations! You just established the identity of about two hundred direct ancestors. Furthermore you've pushed your family tree into the 17th Century with a few lines that seem to push even further into the past. One of these branches leads to a lady named Anne Convent (aka Anne Couvent) who was born in 1601 and died in 1675 (See Figure 5). Later in the book I'll tell you why she is important.

After studying your results I suggest that you return to Rootsweb and look at the first record of the two (the one you decided was inferior): "Compare it to what you downloaded"

The comparison yields one unique branch. "Check the quality" I urge you. You do, and find that it's reasonable and sourced. "Click on the top node of the unique branch and download that GEDCOM."

You do so and repeat the earlier process. This time, however, you click on the duplicate checking functionality immediately following the import into Legacy. A few duplicates are found, and you follow the instructions of the software and merge them. Thirty more direct ancestors are added to your database.

That's the beauty of having French Canadian ancestors: they are well documented. GEDCOM files abound, and Rootsweb is a great place to find them. After this initial success I tell you to return to the original record on Rootsweb so that I can show you something I noticed earlier. "Look at the children of Jean and Grace." Three are listed: "Suzette, Jean Charles, and Joseph Philippe who had the nick name "Pierre".

"Pierre Trudeau?" you reply incredulously "Thee Pierre?" Yes, I nod; the iconic 15th Prime Minister of Canada and father of Justin. Your head snaps back as if someone just shoved you on your forehead.

Step Three – Look for the King and Queen

After you updated your database to include you, your parents, grandparents, I show you how to link your grandparent with the last name Trudeau to Jean Charles Emile. In the pedigree view: right click on Add<Parents<Link to Existing Parents and search for Jean and Grace. When you find them click on Select. Voila! Your family tree now contains over 230 direct ancestors along this branch alone.

"Go back to that second Rootsweb record" I tell you. You click on it and expand the tree view. "Scroll down to the bottom." (See figure 5). I point to a record for Anne Convent/Couvent. "Do you have her in your database?" You downloaded ten generations, and having been born in 1601 she's in danger of having been missed. In the Legacy database (DB), you search for her record and find it. Clicking the pedigree view you find that she in fact belonged to the tenth and final generation downloaded. "Go back to Rootsweb and click on her name."

When you do so her details emerge. She was born in D'Estrees, France in 1601 and died in Quebec City on Christmas Day 1675. You also notice the lengthy list of source citations, the first being Tanguay Volume 1."

"Looks legit" you comment as you continue reading. Then you notice the second citation:

"… research by Roland-Yves Gagne and Laurent Kokanosky have linked Anne Couvent (spelled on many sites Convent) back to Robert, comte d'Artois, son of King Louis VIII"

French-Canadian Roots

CHARLES 1ᵉʳ DUC DE VENDÔME 1515.

"Seriously, King Louis VIII?" you remark.

"Yes. Anne Convent is well known in French Canadian genealogy circles" I reply. "She's what is called a 'royal gateway.' From her you can push your genealogy back in to the middle ages. She was a direct descendent of Charlemagne."

"Who?" your mouth is slight agape.

"Charlemagne. He was a king who lived in the eighth or ninth century. Holy Roman Emperor … He's the ancestor of every European King and Queen. Some say he was the greatest king who ever lived. You've never heard of him?"

You shake your head. You must've been asleep during that part of history class.

This demonstrates step two: look for members of French nobility because they are gateways into the distant past, long before your ancestors arrived in the new world. Aside from Anne Convent some of the names to watch out for are: the Leneuf brothers, Hellene De Belleau, and Catherine De Baillon. A good source of royal gateway people is GFNA - Quebec Royal Descends. They maintain the website Francogene.com/gfna/gfna/998/qrd30.htm that has an extensive list.

For now, though, the important thing is to add Anne Convent's tree to your burgeoning one. Remember that you were only able to download ten generations and she was the tenth. As we're still looking at the Rootsweb record I instruct you to click on Anne's Pedigree view. The screen explodes. Another ten generations of your direct ancestor's pops up, going back to the fourteenth Century. "Grab the GEDCOM" I say.

You're going to have to grab these ten generations, as well as the next ten, and the next ten after that. You'll be downloading a total of forty generations, and hundreds more direct ancestors. By the end of the day your database will have thousands in your pedigree, and you'll know some of your ancestors going back to the year 600 A.D. Still looking at the online pedigree for Anne, I tell you to click on her ancestor Jean VI de Ghistelles who died sometime after 1414. His pedigree explodes before us. Then I tell you to click on Henry I, Margrave of Nordgau who died in 1017. Once again an extensive tree is exposed, this one showing Charlemagne.

"See that guy?" I ask pointing to Charlemagne's grandfather Charles Martel.

French-Canadian Roots

You nod politely with a "so what?" look on your face.

"If it wasn't for him, you'd be Muslim" You turn your head towards me looking for elaboration "in the Battle of Tours he destroyed the Islamic invasion which until that point looked like it was unstoppable. The Muslims had cavalry and the French did not, they were on foot. The strategy he used is still studied in military school".

You notice that Charles Martel was born in 688. "How far back can we go? Can we get back to the time of Christ?"

"Sort of. This is about as far back as we can reliably go. You're talking about a concept called 'descent from antiquity.' You should read about it on Wikipedia. I only know of one for Western Europeans, and it goes through one of the crusader knights."

"Crusaders? Knights?"

"Yes, you'll have a few in your family tree. It's time for me to go home though. Can you download these GEDCOM files on your own?" You answer in the affirmative, so I leave you with your homework. "Tomorrow we'll discuss how to fix 'broken branches' in your tree. Good night."

Step Four – Fixing Broken Branches

The next morning I return. You have dark circles under your eyes – a true sign that obsession is setting in. "Were you up late last night?"

"Yeah. I was just reading about some of these people in my family tree."

"Interesting, eh?"

"Yes. It was still daylight when I started. When I looked up it was night."

"I've been there." Yes, I know what it's like. "Let's have a look at your family tree." With the file open before us, in the pedigree view, I say "Do you see how this line ends at this lady?" I have to stop myself from tapping the screen. I hate it when people tap on my computer screen. "We need to work on that." I'm referring to the dead end.

"Okay" you reply "What do we do?"

"There are a couple of things we can do. We could travel to Montreal to look for her, but that isn't necessary at this point."

"Especially given that she's dead" you remark dryly.

"We can find her records online. We don't need to fly to Montreal. There's an easy way, and if that doesn't work there is another way that's a little harder."

"What's the easy way?"

"Since she lived in the 1700's we can find her on the PRDH"

"What's the PRDH?"

The PRDH is a genealogy project conducted by the University of Montreal. They maintain an online database that is well researched and reliable. However, unlike Rootsweb, you have to pay for the service. Luckily we both have an endless supply of money. This won't cost much though. I grab a coffee from the kitchen while you enter your credit card information.

Returning I set two steaming mugs down on the desk.

"Now what?" you say.

I point my left hand in a go forward motion "See if you can find her." You locate her, and her parents are shown. "Enter the information in Legacy." After you do so, and establish the proper links, I encourage you do be a good genealogist and cite your sources. I show you where you can enter the information on the db.

"Why do I need to cite my sources?" It seems like a waste of time to you. This is just for your purposes.

"So that when you look back at this record, you know how you got it. Plus, one day you may download it to the web as a GEDCOM so that you can help other genealogists."

"Fine." You're perturbed. This feels a little too much like work, but you enter the information. "Now what?"

"Eventually you'll return to Rootsweb to see if there's a GEDCOM for this lady's parents, but for now let's look at another broken link." The next one you look at is your great-great-great grandmother Marie Catherine Longtin. She died in 1778. In vain, you try the PRDH website.

"Nothing. I guess that's it."

"You're going to give up just like that?"

"What else can I do?"

"Ancestry.com"

"But if these guys don't have it, why would Ancestry?"

"Trust me, try their website." You type in the website address and it asks for some of that unlimited money supply you have. After entering your credit card information I instruct you to enter her name, plus that of her husband (your great grandfather) in the query tool for Marriage Records. You enter an approximate year for the marriage that is likely +/- within ten years. You get a direct hit and within moments you're looking at their marriage record. Accompanying the record is a scan of the actual written record of their marriage, February 17, 1749. Not only did they sign the document, but it also bears the

French-Canadian Roots

signatures of their parents. The quality of the scan is excellent as is the penmanship of all the signatories. From this document you can clearly tell who Marie Catherine Longtin's parents were …. Your great great great …. Grandparents. As you look at their signatures your mouth is once again slightly ajar. It's a special moment when you see the handwriting of your ancestor who signed so long ago. You update your database. I leave your house as you're searching Rootsweb for GEDCOM files for the two sets of great-grandparent's you just uncovered. You barely notice me leave.

*****

There are other websites you can use to fix the broken branches of your tree, but when it comes to French Canadian ancestors the PRDH and Ancestry are two of the best.

Expected Results

If you have French Canadian ancestors the method I've
outlined should have two results.

Firstly, with enough diligence, you will determine *every*
French Canadian ancestor born after the year 1600. This
assumes two things: First: all the Branches lead to
individuals that were included in the 1666 Census of New
France. 3,215 Europeans in 538 families were counted, and
invariably almost all French Canadians can traces their
lines to this relatively small group.

The above is true if none of your lines has orphans,
indigenous people, or "late comers" to New France. Recall
that France's dominion over that part of the world lasted
less than a hundred more years. By 1759 New France was
lost to the English never to be recovered. Thus, 1759 is the
last possible year that your French Canadian ancestors
could've immigrated to the new world. Consistently
though, you'll find that they arrived well before that year.

The second result you can expect, especially if all four of
your grand parents were French Canadian, is that some of
your lines lead to "royal gateway" people such as Anne
Convent and you'll be able to push your family tree all the
way back to Charlemagne in the eighth century.

And the final result you can expect is that you'll uncover
several thousand direct ancestors whose management
entails that you have a proper database system such as
Legacy Family Tree. The majority of these records will

have been found with relative ease, thus the decision to invest in proper software at an early stage was prudent.

Discover Your Cousins

Now that you've uncovered a vast number of your direct ancestors you can go one step further. Aside from Trudeau, who are your cousins?

Step One - Finding Targets

You probably know some of your first cousins. You may even know a few second cousins. But amongst your more distant cousins are there any celebrities? Are there any famous political figures? Any infamous relatives that are best left uncovered?

If you know that someone famous has at least some French Canadian ancestry there is a chance that you are related to them if you go far enough back. People that have such

42

ancestors include former U.S. Presidential candidate Hillary Clinton, pop star Justin Bieber, and movie start Angelina Jolie. You might be surprised to find that the Duchess of Cornwall, Camilla Parker Bowles, also has French Canadian ancestors.

Others include pop star Madonna, French Canadian songstress Celine Dion, and NFL Hall of Fame quarterback Brett Favre.

All of the celebrities mentioned above may be related to you. If all four of your grandparents are French Canadian it is almost assured that they are.

Though she does not have French Canadian ancestry the Queen of England, Elizabeth II, does have French ancestors. If you can take your pedigree back far enough you may find a link between the two of you.

Step Two

The process for establishing a direct connection between you and a celebrity is similar to that which you followed when you established our own ancestry. Once you have a target, you have to establish that person's pedigree. Their parents can usually be found on their Wikipedia article. Occasionally even their grandparents are listed. You'll have to be creative on the internet to push their lineage into the nineteenth century.

Step Three

Once you've pushed the target's pedigree into the nineteenth century follow the same steps that you used to establish your own ancestry. Be sure to load the GEDCOM files you discover into your database. Also be wary of duplicate records as you may have many. Run the duplicate checking program of your software after every load.

Step Four

After you've discovered the celebrity's lineage, downloaded it into your database, and removed duplicate records you are ready for the final step: establishing your direct relationship with them.

To do this use the relationship checking function of your genealogy software (the better ones have such as Legacy have it).

Expected Results

If you're hunch turns out to be correct you'll find such a connection. Typically amongst people with French Canadian ancestry it will be somewhere between eighth and tenth cousins. Occasionally it will be even closer. For example Angelina Jolie is my fifth cousin. We are both direct descendents of my maternal great-great grandfather who died in 1838.

If you count Queen Elizabeth II as a cousin it's quite likely a far more remote relationship; in my case she is a 14th cousin, almost beyond distant.

English Roots

To the extent that your family tree is amongst the first pioneers to settle in what is now French Canada you will find two points of intersection with English ancestors.

Kidnapped!

The first point where your French Canadian tree will intersect with those of the English is with individuals kidnapped during one of the many hostilities between the two colonial archenemies (refer to the section in this book called "The New World"). Both sides did it, but the relevance to us is with those British-American individuals who chose not to return to their native land after they were set free.

An example of this occurred as a result of the 1704 raid during Queen Anne's War when French and Native forces attacked the English frontier settlement at Deerfield, Massachusetts taking 112 settlers captive to Montreal. Some died along the way and sixty were later redeemed (ransomed by family and community). In this period, the

English were involved in similar raids against French villages where they were doing their own abducting and ransoming.

Some of the captives, however, were not ransomed and they remained by choice for the rest of their lives. This is particularly true of many of the younger captives who were adopted into French Canadian society. Thirty six Deerfield captives, mostly children and teenagers at the time of the raid, remained permanently. Those who stayed were not compelled by force, but rather by newly formed religious ties and family bonds. Captive experience was largely dictated by gender as well as age. Young women most easily and readily assimilated into French Canadian society. Nine girls remained as opposed to only five boys. These choices reflect the larger frontier pattern of incorporation of young women into Canadian society. These young women remained, not because of compulsion, fascination with the outdoor adventure, or the strangeness of life in a foreign society, but because they transitioned into established lives in new communities and formed bonds of family, religion, and language. In fact, more than half of young female captives who remained settled in Montreal where "the lives of these former Deerfield residents differed very little in their broad outlines from their former neighbors." Whether in New France or in Deerfield these women generally were part of frontier agricultural communities where they tended to marry in their early twenties and have six or seven children.

French-Canadian Roots

Note: The previous paragraph is based on the book "Captors and Captives: The 1704 French and Indian Raid on Deerfield." by Evan Haefeli and Kevin Sweeney.

Once you find an ancestor who started life off as a kidnapping victim, you'll have a pedigree that could lead to some interesting characters from early American history. In my case it led to the Salem Witch Trials.

The Norman Conquest of England

The second point at which your family tree will intersect with those of the English results from William the Conquerors conquest of England in 1066. William was a Frenchman who was also the Duke of Normandy on France's Northwest coast. The result of his victory in the Battle of Hastings was several hundred years of Norman rule over England, creating a situation where the official language of the royal court of England was in fact French. Even after the Norman influence over England ended (after several centuries) the English royal family continued to marry with those of the French.

The result is that your pedigree, if you've been able to find "royal gateway" ancestors among the French Canadian pioneers (e.g. Anne Convent and the Leneuf family), will intersect with the English during the late middle ages. Undoubtedly you'll count the prodigious King Edward the First of England, a man of French descent with numerous offspring, as your ancestor. He is portrayed below left as the villain in the movie Braveheart.

Amongst the Norman elite of England were Richard the Lionhearted and Eleanor of Aquitaine, people you are likely to find in your family tree. You'll also find the tyrant King John, who was forced to sign the Magna Carat in 1215.

There is also another interesting byproduct of extending your family tree to the Norman/French rulers of Britain: using your genealogical software you can establish your precise relationship to Queen Elizabeth, Prince William, Princess Diana, and the rest of the present monarchy of the United Kingdom. Just don't expect to be invited to the next coronation as you're likely on the order of a 14th or 15th cousin.

Additional Resources

Aside from what I've mentioned in this book there are plenty of other resources that are worthwhile. The Family History Library in downtown Salt Lake City is fantastic. Like most of the archives I've come across their records have been digitalized and are available on the internet. The real value is in their huge genealogical book library. It is several floors, although the French Canadian section is relatively small compared to other sections. The staff is extremely helpful if you need help in your search.

An additional website is also worth mentioning. It is called "Jamie Allen's Family Tree & Ancient Genealogical Allegations." Assuming you find a "royal gateway" ancestor in your tree (if all four of your grandparents were French Canadian it is assured), Jamie's portal will both entertain and may even assist you. Very few of the pioneers of New France on the site, but when you have a "gateway" ancestor this site can help you navigate the royal world before 1600. You can compare your tree to Jamie's for accuracy and to help when you've hit a road block. Be cautioned that this website is not error free, but it in most respects it is reasonable. You can find it at Fabpedigree.com.

You Should Go

The majority of your research will be on the internet. I once went to the Charente Maritime Archives in La Rochelle France, excited about the discoveries I was about to make. There I found a record of my ancestor's wedding in 1631. I was dismayed when I saw a stamp on it indicating that it had been scanned and was now preserved in the digital archive of the Church of Latter Day Saints (LDS). Since Ancestry.com embeds the LDS's records on their site, this meant that I didn't have to travel all the way to France to see this. Later at the hotel I was staying at I got on my computer and confirmed what I suspected: it was available on the internet. Every record I found there was in fact available on the web. From this perspective the trip seemed like a waste of time.

But it wasn't.

The true value in going to France, as well as to Quebec, is that you gain a context for the dry records that you're compiling. For example, before I went to France I didn't fully realize the extent to which my ancestors were Huguenots.

French-Canadian Roots

The Huguenots were a French Protestant denomination that is virtually extinct due to war and persecution. It's quite likely that the vast majority of your ancestors came from families that were members. The realization came after visiting the Huguenot Museum in La Rochelle. By going to France you get a sense for what your ancestors left behind. By going to Quebec you get a sense for what they left for. This will enrich your understanding of your ancestors and make you a better genealogist.

If you do go to France the city of La Rochelle is a must. When New France was lost to the British in 1759 the economy of this beautiful city died, so the downtown is essentially as it was back in the 18th and 17th century. Explore the surrounding countryside and nearby St. Jean D'Angely as it also produced many of your forbearers. Visit the Charente Maritime archives not so much for their records, but for the books that they have.

French-Canadian Roots

You should also visit Quebec. You'll find archives in Montreal, Quebec City, and other places. However, the place you *must* visit is Old Quebec. When you go there you are stepping back in time. In my case the home of the first Campagna born in the new world still stands, solidly built in the year 1700. You'll make similar discoveries.

Ancestral Adventures

If you take a trip to your ancestral homeland you'll enjoy many interesting experiences that you'll never get if you spend all of your days on a computer in the comfort of your home. To date, the story that follows is my most intriguing.

The Séance

"Que fais tu ici?" the lady asked. She was short, gray hair arranged in a bun, and wore a long flowery dress with no sleeves. She had just caught me snooping around her place on this hot August day.

I asked her in my limited French if she spoke English, to which she replied "Non." My phone had a translation app, so I had her repeat her question into it. "What are you doing here?" The app spit out.

"My ancestors lived in this house." I said into my machine. Then I listened as the machine made me comprehensible.

We were standing outside her cute little maison in Southwest France. It was a long thin two story home, with green shutters, crème colored walls with a hint of yellow, and a red tile roof. The tile was the same as I had back on the roof of my home back in the desert of California, which told me that this area was no stranger to heat. Two large baby blue planters guarded the front door, each with a large ficus bush. An assortment of potted plants was strewn about the compound, but it was by no means messy. The farm upon which the house stood was immaculate.

French-Canadian Roots

I had attracted her attention by peaking through the iron gates that led into the compound, taking photographs, when she finally decided to engage me from the other side of the metal bars.

"I am Lawrence. My ancestors used to live here." I repeated into my translator, not sure if it was accurate and hoping that it didn't misinterpret and produce something offensive or ridiculous. This time she slowly nodded yes, confirming that she understood. Then I hit the jackpot. "My great grandmother died in this house."

At this she became excited and talked directly into the translator. "My name is Helene. I am a medium. I can speak to the dead."

At this I mirrored her excitement, but not because of my long dead ancestor. I thought of the son I had lost to cancer two years earlier. The lady asked me if I'd like to attend a séance. Pushing aside my skepticism I accepted her invitation. "Demain" she said. *Tomorrow.*

French-Canadian Roots

It didn't matter whether she could communicate with the departed or not; I had just been invited inside the last house my ancestors occupied in Europe. I thought of the photo opportunities I would get. But in the back of my mind skepticism was waning: I wanted to talk to my son.

We chatted for a little while longer and concluded our discussion with an appointment at 4pm tomorrow.

Sometimes in America we say "arrivederci". This is what I said to her and she understood the Italian way of saying good bye. This made her smile.

Only later did I think that it was strange to be invited into a stranger's house, at least by North American standards. Was I going to find myself in a boiling pot surrounded by onions, carrots, and seasoning? Those thoughts were

French-Canadian Roots

dispelled by Marguerite, the innkeeper at the hotel I was staying at. She knew this lady and vouched for her.

So the next day I went back to the farmhouse. Standing on the other side of the gate, I pushed the intercom button. "Bonjour Helene. Laurent ici" I said when she answered. As I mentioned before, I knew a tiny amount of French including the equivalent to my name. Even this exchange was pushing my limits. But it was enough: an electric motor slid the gate to the side allowing me to pass.

She met me at the door and invited me in. I used the translator to say "Marguerite from the hotel says hello." For safety's sake I wanted her to know that a third party knew I was here. The medium smiled and said something I didn't understand. I just nodded as if I did. She motioned me to sit at the kitchen table. As I looked around the kitchen I noticed the thick open beams of the ceiling, hundreds of years old. Then I felt the warmth produced by the knick knacks on her shelves and the family heirlooms that surrounded me. I could almost see my own ancestors in this room.

My imagination took me to my distant great great … grand mother, dying of a disease while only in her early 30's, the medicine men of her day unable to come to grips with what was killing her. She was surrounded by her children, one of whom would continue a line that would extend all the way to the present, to me.

Now I was standing here in her house, deep in the heart of southwest France, with a person who claimed to be able to communicate with the dead.

"Asseyez-vous", she said. *Sit down.*

I placed my translation device on the table between us. The modern day lady of the house said "Avec qui souhaitez-vous parler?" *With whom do you wish to speak?*

I thought of my son, but remained mute. She looked at me for a moment longer before I spoke. "My great grandmother's name was Madeleine Lemay. She's the one who died in this house." In truth several "great, great, great's" needed to be added to the word grandmother to be accurate.

A small violet box sat on the table and she lifted the lid off. From it she pulled out a chain with a pendulum in the shape of an elongated heart at the end of it. Both were made of gold. She held the end of the chain high and let the pendulum swing about four inches from the surface of the dark wooden table. Then she said in French "Once I make contact with your grandmother she will answer through this pendulum. Clockwise means her answer is yes, counter means no. Do you understand?"

I nodded in the affirmative.

She let the jewelry dangle for a minute and then said "She's here. What would you like to ask her?"

"What did she die of?" I asked in English.

Helene's eyes were closed and her face tight as she focused. At my question she opened them, still relaxed but with a trace of irritation. "She can only answer yes or no through the movement of the pendulum." She closed her eyes again with her hand still held above the table.

"Did you die in an accident?"

Counter clockwise movement. *No.*

"Did you die from an illness?" *Yes.*

"Was it cancer?" *No.* "Was it tuberculosis?" *Yes.*

All the while this dialog was taking place through my translator. It wasn't nearly as smooth as it would've been had we spoken the same language. I should've asked the question. "Is this the clumsiest séance ever?" But I didn't. My mama taught me to be polite, and I truly did appreciate Helene's hospitality. I was a complete stranger sitting in her house receiving a gift.

I looked up toward the open beams of the ceiling and said "Thank you Grandma Madeleine. We still remember you down here on Earth. Say hello to Grandpa Denis." Then my gaze shifted back to my medium whose eyes were still closed. "I would like to talk to someone else." I asked

French-Canadian Roots

Helene. She looked at me. "I would like to talk to my son. He died two years ago. His name was Wyatt." As she nodded she closed her eyes.

The pendulum swung, back and forth. Neither clockwise nor counter, just from side to side. A minute went by and she said "Demander." Ask.

"Are you okay Wyatt?" Clockwise movement.

"Have you seen grandpa?" Clockwise.

"Are you happy?" The pendulum stopped moving. Almost like an invisible hand had reached out and grabbed it.

"Are you in a good place?" Clockwise.

"Do you miss someone?" Clockwise.

"Me?" Counter clockwise. I'm glad he's not missing me, sort of.

"Your mother?" Counter.

I knew all along. "Emily?" The pendulum began a rapid clockwise rotation. By the time he died at 22 years old, he had been with Emily for six years. They were completely in love and now they were apart.

"One day, the two of you will be together again Wyatt." It wasn't a question, but still the pendulum swung in the affirmative. "We miss you and love you. Say hello to grandpa." Then I touched Helene's arm. "Thank you."

"Did you get your questions answered," She said.

French-Canadian Roots

"I did" and thanked her again. Always the translator made us comprehensible to one another. We both rose from our seats as she put the pendulum back in its purple box. "May I take a few photos?" She told me that I could and I photographed the kitchen and living room, and then the farmyard outside. After that I returned to my hotel to enjoy a sumptuous feast in its idyllic little restaurant. The Bordeaux wine was exquisite.

I've been to France three times, and Quebec twice. My adventures in my ancestral homelands have been many, but of all my experiences the séance was the most intriguing.

Conclusion

Be thankful that you're French Canadian; your genealogical record is one of the most complete in the world, you just have to compile it. Appreciate that your ancestors colonized a world almost as alien to them as Mars is to us. Remember your ancestors who died in the effort to give their children a better life. If you speak French (in addition to English), be thankful for that. It will make your search that much easier. If you speak French, make sure to teach your children the language. If you don't speak French I encourage you to find a French immersion program for your children's education.

About the Author

Lawrence Compagna is a Canadian/American genealogist. He was born on a brisk winter day in Cold Lake, Canada to French Canadian parents. It was on a Friday the 13th. Ignoring superstition he chooses to live his life as if it is lucky, traveling the world with pen in hand. He is an author, management consultant, genealogist, Chartered Professional Accountant (CPA), and father of three who now lives in Southern California. Visit the author's Facebook page at: fb.me/LawrenceCompagna

The author's blog can be found at Compagna.xyz

Send a message to the author via Facebook at: m.me/LawrenceCompagna

Visit the author's genealogy Facebook page at: http://tinyurl.com/Larrys-Genealogy and TREEZ.XYZ

A database with over 65,000 of his ancestors can be found at http://tinyurl.com/Larrys-Index

http://www.facebook.com/Lawren

fb.me/LawrenceCompagna

The Journey
http://www.amazon.com/dp/B0748R

gick Genealogy

http://www.lulu.com/...
frenc.../paperlack/produc
(French Canadian Geneal

" Mind Blowing Methods"